MOTHER NATURE GOES NUTS!

Amazing Natural Disasters

KLUTZ®

TABLE OF DISASTERS

"I told you kids to stop hanging on the rim!"

On the morning of April 3, 1974, the students of Meadowlawn Elementary School in Monticello, Indiana, practiced their severe storm drill. It turned out to be excellent timing. Just after 5 pm that afternoon, a tornado ripped off the school's roof and left this calling card in the playground.

TORNADO 1
HOOP 0

Portrait of a Monster

Not all tornadoes are created equal.

Take this one pictured here, a tornado that hit Hesston, Kansas, in 1990. On the Fujita scale (see sidebar), it's an F-5, making it both an official monster and an extremely rare beast. Ninety percent of all tornadoes are in the F-1 – F-3 category. It's only when conditions are perfect that an F-5 develops. But when it happens, the result is like a combination freight train and bomb, a perfect storm.

A few of the more notorious F-5s are:

• The Flint, Michigan, tornado of June 8, 1953. The storm system that produced it moved on and spawned another tornado that hit Worcester, Massachusetts, the next day, for a true double whammy.

• The Waco, Texas, tornado of May 11, 1953. It demolished, among other things, a six-story furniture store and put to rest the old Native American belief that a tornado would never hit Waco.

• The Super Outbreak of April 3, 1974, in which 148 tornadoes hit 13 states. Six of those tornadoes were F-5 monsters.

RATE THE TORNADO

Scientists use the Fujita scale to rate tornadoes from F-1 to F-5, based on the damage they do.

F-1: Winds 73–112 mph (117–180 km/h)
Chimneys, tree branches and signs are at risk.

F-2: Winds 113–157 mph (181–253 km/h)
Pushes moving cars off roads and mobile homes off foundations. May destroy garages.

F-3: Winds 158–206 mph (254–332 km/h)
Tears roofs off houses, snaps or uproots trees, demolishes mobile homes.

F-4: Winds 207–260 mph (333–419 km/h)
Tears roofs and walls off houses, overturns trains and uproots many trees.

F-5: Winds 261 mph (420 km/h) and over
Lifts houses off foundations and carries them, makes cars fly through the air, strips the bark off trees.

The Fujita scale is named after its creator, the late Dr. T. Theodore Fujita. Here, he is pictured watching a mini-tornado made in his lab.

Flying Roofs and Air-Plucked Chickens

A roofless house is a fairly common sight in the track of a tornado. The reason? A combination of carpentry and aerodynamics.

Peaked roofs behave like poorly designed aircraft wings. The wind flows over them, reducing the pressure on top, giving the roof an upward lift. If the wind is strong enough, the nails will pull up and away goes the roof.

AN EXPERIMENT

Huff and Puff and...

...prove that moving air can lift things. Hold a piece of paper by one end right in front of your mouth. Blow over the top and the drooping end will lift up.

Chickens that survive tornadoes are often found in a semi-plucked condition. The phenomenon is so common that one experimenter (in 1842) suggested that the strength of a tornado be rated depending on the number of feathers it manages to strip from its chicken victims. He even went so far as to launch a dead (but still feathered) chicken out of a cannon. Unfortunately, the chicken ended up in small, hard-to-find pieces, making conclusions about its feathers a little hard to figure. Modern scientists have since dropped the theory because chickens, when frightened, shed feathers all on their own, even without a tornado.

Pre-tornado

Survivor

(barely)

Post-tornado

Why Is This Man Smiling?

The Navy once ran a series of experiments to find out what happens when pilots eject from their aircraft at flight speeds. In the first round, a mannequin with a leather mask was placed before a special wind machine and the dial turned up to 300 mph (about 480 km/h). (Coincidentally, this is about the top measured speed in a tornado.) The mask ripped to shreds. In the second round, a volunteer stood in for the mannequin. His face, you'll be relieved to know, stayed on and even returned to normal.

Tess Bentley had only a few seconds before her home in Haines City, Florida, was hit by a tornado. She used those precious seconds to dive into her closet ("The closet actually came to me more than I came to it"). The storm ripped her mobile home off its foundation, gave it a ride, turned it upside-down and dumped it onto her neighbor's. Injuries? Nothing too serious. Even her porcelain angel collection survived ("I truly believe I have an angel watching over me").

Amazing Survival Stories

We know of only one person who can answer the question: "What does the interior of a tornado look like?" Kansas farmer Will Keller reached the door of his storm cellar only a few seconds before the twister reached him. In the instant before he closed the door, he had a glimpse of something very few have ever lived to tell about: the insides of a tornado. He reported a screaming, hollow tube made of black swirling clouds, with lightning that zigzagged from side to side.

The Homemade
Tornado Machine

By carefully following these directions, you can build a machine that will launch tiny twisters at people across the room. And irritate them.

1. Start with a cardboard tube. The best kind are oatmeal containers. Get rid of the oatmeal somehow. Then, cut a small circular hole in the bottom. Put it dead center, and make it about 1 inch (2.5 cm) across.

2. Cover the other end of the container (the open end) with a sheet of thin rubber. (We used an old balloon.) Secure it tightly in place with a rubber band — it should be as tight as a drum.

rubber band

balloon

oatmeal box

cut a 1-inch hole

3. You're all set. Point your tube at some unsuspecting soul across the room. Snap the rubber bottom by pulling back on it and releasing. A tiny twister will come out of the other end and, if your aim is any good, hit your victim with a little puff.

SAFETY NOTE: Adult supervision is required for this activity. Have an adult help cut the hole in the cardboard. Balloons are a choking hazard, and children under 8 can suffocate on uninflated balloons.

doughnut of compressed air

HOW COME IT WORKS?

When you snap the rubber on the bottom of the tube, you launch a bullet of compressed air out the hole on the other side. The confusing bit? The bullet gets turned inside out when it collides with the still air of the room.

An analogy? The doughnut hole becomes the doughnut. The doughnut stays intact as it travels because it's made of spinning air. Technically speaking, the doughnut is a tornado grabbing its own tail.

At 1:30 in the afternoon on Friday, August 16, 1993, a tornado touched down beside the front door of the Wal-Mart in Colonial Heights, Virginia, and proceeded to carve a neat slice of near-total destruction through the diapers, lingerie and Kathy Lee Gifford Collection. Moments later, the storm lifted off near the back exit. One employee said it felt like two seconds, but was probably about fifteen. To see what the store looked like afterward, turn the page.

WAL-MART

AFTER TORNADO

Storm Chasers

They call them "storm chasers," and when tornado season starts, they keep their trucks ready and their radios tuned to the weather station.

At the first tornado warning, they're off and running — *toward* the sighting. It's a high-thrill sport. If you're interested, you can sign up with an outfitter whose promise reads: "Travel with us, where the weather *really* sucks."

Tornado Alley About one-third of the world's tornadoes occur in this part of the USA.

Dust Devils

On a really hot day, the sun beats down on the ground and heats it like a frying pan. The air directly above this hot spot also heats up and will sometimes spiral up toward the cooler air (obeying the hot-air-rises rule). If the ground is loose sand, the spiraling wind picks it up, making a dust devil.

Big dust devils hundreds of feet tall are fairly rare but mini-devils are around all the time, often powered by no more than the wind turning the corner of a building.

A Hail of a Storm

The violent thunderstorms that produce tornadoes sometimes also spit out hail. Hail forms when bits of dust or pollution get whisked up and down in the strong updrafts of a thunderstorm and are coated with layer upon layer of ice.

Some hailstones are whoppers. On June 22, 2003, the town of Aurora, Nebraska, was thumped with hailstones the size of volleyballs. Even bigger ones, about the size of pumpkins, fell in Bangladesh in 1986.

Waterspouts

▲ A tornado-like swirling column of water is called a waterspout. Sometimes these form when land tornadoes pass across water and suck up a drink. But most often, waterspouts start when swirling winds from above stir up a patch of the water's surface. If the winds continue, they can build into a fully formed spout. Waterspouts have been known to pick up fish and even small boats, lift them out of the water and give them a spin.

Oklahoma City, Tornado Town USA

It's an honor most cities would rather *not* have — City Most Likely To Be Hit By a Tornado. And the winner is… Oklahoma City, Oklahoma. Since 1893, when records were first kept there, it has been struck by tornadoes an unbelievable 193 times.

HURRICANES

What IS It about Florida and Hurricanes?

FLORIDA
FRANCES
DMV

Over the last century, more than 60 hurricanes have struck the state of Florida, making it the undisputed, world champion, hurricane hotspot. The storms can come in from three directions — south, east and west — usually during hurricane season, from June to November. On average, Florida gets hit once every two years.

But that's on average. At the extreme end of the records, you can find the year 2004, when three full-fledged hurricanes hit the state within 21 days. It was an unprecedented string that left residents with billions of dollars of damage and scientists with a difficult but deeply important meteorological question, which can best be paraphrased as, "What's going on?"

Orlando

Tampa

Miami

Scientists expect that global warming will create more and stronger hurricanes, but they're not at all sure that this was the cause of the 2004 hurricanes. It's more likely it was just plain old bad luck.

How to Cook a Hurricane

If you think of the tropical seas as steaming pots of water cooked by the sun and stirred by the turning of the Earth itself, you'll understand the basic recipe for hurricanes. Hurricanes are born and sustained by warm water and they die within a few days of leaving it.

Most Atlantic Ocean hurricanes start as storm "seedlings" that form in late summer off the coast of West Africa. These storms travel west, often growing in strength as they feed on the warm ocean water.

The winds start to spiral as a result of the earth's rotation. The storm grows and grows, finally hitting wind speeds of 74 mph (119 km/h) or more. It is now officially a hurricane.

Cross Section of a Hurricane

Cooled air plunges down to be warmed.

At the center is an eye of calm.

Bands of rain and intense wind spiral around the eye.

Air warmed by the ocean spirals upward.

Hurricane birds, the Lockheed P-3 Orion

Why You Don't Want to Fly in These Planes

In 1943, an Air Force pilot by the name of Joseph Duckworth decided (all on his own) to do what no one had ever done before: fly an airplane straight through the outer wall of a hurricane and right into its eye. His single-engine trainer was thrown around the sky like a toy, but Duckworth managed to get into the calm of the storm's center where he reported blue sky above and an incredibly tortured sea below.

Duckworth got a medal for his flight, and a small band of derring-do pilots were recruited by the National Weather Service to invent the fine art of hurricane flying while gathering meteorological data.

One veteran hurricaner, Commander David Turner, was once interviewed about a particularly rough mission into Hurricane Edith: "It was a bit more than the ordinary flight. In fact, we got the living daylights beaten out of us. We were jerked around so violently that I couldn't tell which way was up — all the dials were going nuts." Shortly after landing,

Turner re-fueled and went right back up ("We just wanted to verify it had been that rough"). He was once asked why he volunteered for the flights (the money isn't that good); "Oh, it's interesting work," he replied.

Another military pilot, Bill Rankin, showed how you could fly even without the benefit of an airplane (something that people used to think was impossible).

Rankin's jet lost an engine over Virginia in 1959 and he had to eject right over the heart of a violent thunderstorm. The moment his parachute opened, he found (to his surprise) that he was going up (not down) at a terrific rate. Here is how he described the experience:

"I went soaring up and up... buffeted in all directions — up, down, sideways, clockwise, counterclockwise, over and over. I was stretched, slammed and pounded like a bag of flesh crashing into concrete. Meanwhile, it was raining so hard, I thought I would drown in mid-air."

Bill Rankin's airplane-less stormy flight appears to be unique. At least, no one else has ever come back down to Earth in a condition to talk about any similar experience.

The Story of Hurricane Camille and

When civil defense authorities issue a hurricane evacuation order, there are always a few thrill-seekers who deliberately ignore the warnings. Instead, they plant themselves right in the hurricane's path and hope to get a really close look at really big weather.

Molly Blackenstone (not her real name) was one of those people. In 1969 she and a group of about 20 friends decided to disregard evacuation warnings and gather for a "hurricane party" on the third floor of their apartment building. Not a good idea.

Hurricane Camille was a Class V hurricane, with core winds of 200 mph (about 320 km/h). In a sudden change of direction, the storm took dead-aim at their little town of Pass Christian, Mississippi.

the Former Richelieu Apartment Building

Molly never even got to the party. She and her husband were still in their apartment when the picture window blew out ("We heard an awful popping sound"). Moments later, both of them had their shoulders pressed against the door, trying to keep out the wind and water.

It was hopeless. The entire building began to rock ("It felt like we were in a boat"). Molly's last glimpse of her apartment

building came as she swam through her second-story window, washed out on the storm surge.

Exactly what happened next is not entirely clear. Molly was found in a tree more than 5 miles (8 km) from the former Richelieu apartment building, miraculously alive. In an interview afterward, she stated that during the next hurricane watch, "I'm leaving along with the rest of them."

The Hurricane Hall of Fame and Facts

The University of Miami mascot is the ibis, which is the last bird to leave before a hurricane arrives and the first bird to come back when it leaves.

Strongest Hurricane of All Time?

Hurricane Gilbert had recorded winds of 218 mph (350 km/h) when it struck Northern Mexico in 1988. The pressure inside Gilbert was the lowest ever recorded by meteorologists.

Deadliest Hurricane in North American History?

Probably the hurricane that hit Galveston, Texas, on September 8, 1900. As the winds built up early in the day, people streamed to the beach to see the huge waves. A surge of water pushed ahead of the hurricane and soon children were playing in flooded yards. But the fun stopped with the arrival of the full force of the hurricane and the flooding. In 24 hours, the entire city was underwater, leaving 15 percent of the population dead.

Galveston was rebuilt. A huge sea wall was constructed. And 2000 buildings were jacked up above sea level, with the land filled in under them, so that such destruction could never happen again.

Jupiter's Great Red Spot is approximately three Earths wide.

Shown to scale

Biggest Hurricane of All?

On the planet Jupiter, they know how to make hurricanes. Or at least things that look like hurricanes. The Jovian whirlwind shown here, called the Great Red Spot, was first seen by Galileo 300 years ago. It's still spinning today.

The Name Game

For a long time, all hurricanes were given girls' names. That changed in 1979 with the first "boy" hurricane — Bob. Today, official policy is to alternate.

A really big hurricane may have its name "retired" (never used again) — as when a sports hero retires and takes his jersey number with him.

P.S. Hurricanes are called typhoons in other parts of the world. Both hurricanes and typhoons are tropical cyclones.

Q: Are there hurricanes at the equator?

A: The experts said no —

The equator has the warm waters that can give birth to hurricanes, but not the spinning winds. Then, on December 27, 2001, the experts were proved wrong. Typhoon Vamei developed over the equator in the South China Sea near Singapore.

Now You Know Why They Call Them Mobile Homes.

Mobile homes have a mysterious sort of reputation for attracting tornadoes and hurricanes since the after-storm news shows are often filled with pictures of flipped and smashed RVs. But the real story has less to do with the Twilight Zone and more to do with building codes. Mobile homes don't have foundations and make very poor storm shelters.

What Happens When a Hurricane Hits a Children's Book Publishing Company?

Florida has had its fill of doom-and-gloom weather forecasters with predictions of disaster that never materialized. But on August 13, 2004, all that changed as Hurricane Charley stunned South and Central Florida with a wicked left uppercut that knocked down thousands of trees and left millions of residents without power. Many of us at Scholastic in Lake Mary, Florida, were caught flat-footed. Despite dire warnings, we just knew this was going to be one more in a long series of false alarms. Sure, we'd get some wind and rain, but we'd had daily thunderstorms do more damage than recent hurricanes. But Charley was a wake-up call. Many of us couldn't even leave our homes. And it came at one of our busiest times of the year: In just a few days, dozens of book experts and publishing companies were gathering in Orlando to select the books that would appear in the upcoming Scholastic Book Fairs.

We had hardly had a chance to regroup with new appointments and travel plans when Hurricane Frances threw a very slow right hook at us on September 5, causing extensive flooding. And finally, wandering Hurricane Jeanne hit us with a strong right cross three weeks later, disrupting school schedules and wreaking havoc with our Book Fair events. Charley, Frances and Jeanne were the second, fourth and eighth costliest hurricanes in U.S. history. **OUCH!**

(For the answer to the related question, "What would happen to a children's book publishing company if it were hit by an earthquake?" turn to page 25.)

If you could stand back and give the planet a good whack, the entire globe would vibrate with the impact. Assuming you really hauled off and hit it, people in New York would feel the vibrations even though you brought the hammer down in Missouri. The reason? The rocky crust of the planet makes the Earth ring like a bell and an impact anywhere will send waves shaking around the globe.

Although nobody's banging it with a hammer, the Earth gets a giant whack or three every year from its own shifting crust, which is made of massive plates that jostle each other for position. Every time the plates shift and grind against each other, the shock waves travel outward and turn what is really a local kind of fender-bender into something with much larger reverberations.

EARTHQUAKES

Lie on your stomach for a second and put your lower jaw flat on the ground. Close your eyes. Do you feel any groundshake or vibrations? No? It didn't work for us either. But for snakes it works quite well. Footsteps of animals walking nearby will create ground vibrations. By resting its lower jaw on the ground, a snake can sense footsteps from as far away as 25 yards (23m).

Three bones in your middle ear evolved from the jawbones of extinct animals and may help to explain why in the movies, Indian scouts can tell you how many days to the next wagon train by putting their ear to the ground.

The reason any of this works is simple: The planet is a rocky, dirty bell and wagon trains, footsteps, earthquakes, dropped vases and on-coming stampedes all ring it to one degree or another.

Kobe, Japan
January 17, 1995

Where Do Earthquakes Happen?

Think of the Earth as a giant baseball. The seams mark the edges of the plates that make up the Earth's crust. Earthquakes happen along the seams.

In all, there are seven huge plates and many smaller ones. The biggest one, about where you see the seams here, is the Pacific plate. It's the source of California's, Japan's and Latin America's earthquakes.

THE OUTHOUSE EARTHQUAKE

Scientists use an instrument called a seismograph to record the strength of an earthquake. Stand up right now and leap into the air. When you land, a wave of energy will travel through the Earth's crust.

If a seismograph is nearby, the wave will be recorded by a needle tracing on a piece of paper. The "wiggle" it creates is called a seismogram.

The United States Geological Survey keeps one seismograph in the pit of an outhouse. The bump you see in the seismogram below was recorded when the door to the outhouse was slammed shut. (This is a true story.)

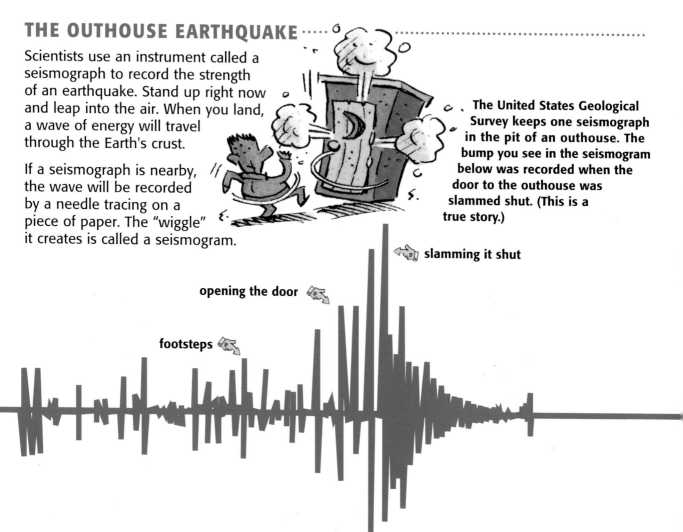

slamming it shut

opening the door

footsteps

Earthquakes Come In 3 Styles

The plates of the Earth's crust are straining against one another in constant gridlock. When the strain breaks, the movement is sharp and sudden. The damage to the crust is seen along faults.

PULLING APART

Plates can pull apart or get pushed apart by hot liquid material surging up from under the Earth's crust. Africa's Great Rift Valley is one place this has happened. Millions of years from now, the movement of the plates may rip the continent of Africa in two along this rift.

HEAD-ON COLLISION

When plates collide, the edges sometimes crumple up into mountain ranges. Or one plate can dive under the other. Sounds smooth but it isn't. Plates can get stuck and energy builds until it is finally released in an earthquake.

SIDESWIPE

A sideswipe means two plates are trying to slide by each other. They stick and grind and it's energy build-up time again. California's San Andreas fault is one example of sideswiping plates. Major earthquakes have rumbled California along this fault.

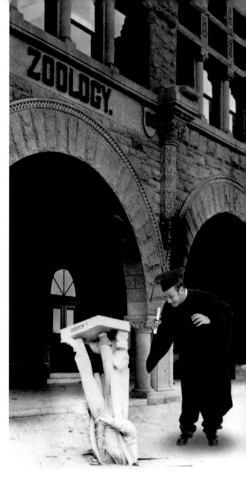

A Before & After Earthquake Photo Album

◀ **BEFORE**   **AFTER** ▶

In this picture, a statue on the Stanford University campus was knocked down by the 1906 San Francisco earthquake. (P.S. The statue was of Louis Agassiz, a vocal opponent of evolution. As someone remarked at the time, "Agassiz was better in the abstract than in the concrete.")

P.S. We cheated and added the graduate to these pictures. But the story is true.

◀ **BEFORE**   **AFTER** ▶

In earthquake country, putting buildings on stilts to allow for ground level parking is bad design. The stilts tend to buckle when the quake hits. Building codes in Los Angeles (home to this building) and throughout California have been toughened since the 1994 Northridge quake, making this kind of construction illegal.

◀ **BEFORE**   **AFTER** ▶

Assuming they aren't on an overpass (or under a building like this one was), cars are pretty good earthquake shelters. Thousands of motorists simultaneously pulled over during the California Loma Prieta quake in 1989 and checked their tires, mistaking the earthquake for nothing more than a flat.

EARTHQUAKE *Trivia*

Fire!

Fires fed by broken gas mains roared out of control in San Francisco the night after the quake of 1989. The section of the city shown here is built on unstable debris and landfill (some of which was created by the 1906 earthquake). The soil liquefied in a way that solid bedrock cannot, and the damage here was the most extensive of anywhere in the city.

Roaches to the Rescue

Trained rescue dogs are often too big to crawl through the worst parts of collapsed buildings in search of survivors. So, Japanese scientists have outfitted roaches with backpacks containing battery-powered radios and mini-microphones. Their hope? Launch squadrons of Rescue Roaches into the buildings and monitor their radios for sounds of survivors. We are not making this up.

Let Sleeping Elephants Lie

Long before modern science figured out what was really going on, there were many, many theories about what caused earthquakes (nobody who lives in earthquake country ignores them). In India, at one time, people believed that eight strong elephants held up the Earth. If one got sleepy and laid down for a nap, the Earth shook.

Do-It-Yourself Earthquake

What would happen if billions of disciplined Chinese got into a crouch and, at a nation-wide broad-casted signal, leapt into the air all at once? Would the impact of their landing be enough to send a shock wave through the Earth's crust and trigger North American earthquake faults? This intriguing question was investigated in 1969 by a couple of Earth scientists whose results were reported in TIME Magazine. The answer is no. You may sleep easy again.

December 26, 2004

Tsunami Strikes Asia & Africa

INDIAN OCEAN

Dec. 26, 2004 — On December 26, 2004, the worst tsunami ever recorded hit coastal towns all over southeast Asia and parts of Africa, flattening homes and sweeping people and belongings out to sea.

An earthquake in the Indian Ocean (at the red dot on this map) started the tsunami. The earthquake thrust up the seafloor, forcing the water above it up too. The bulge of water fanned out in a series of huge waves which destroyed everything in their path.

Hour after hour, the tsunami waves rippled outward, slamming into islands and other land forms.

Finally, seven hours after it started, the tsunami hit the coast of Africa. In all, more than 200,000 people were killed in more than 10 countries.

Deadliest Natural Disaster in Almost 30 Years

Earthquake-triggered tsunami waves hitting Kammale temple in Phuket, Thailand.

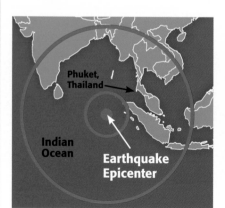

28

First Person
One Survivor's Story

PHUKET, THAILAND
Dec. 26, 2004 — Troy Husum had left the cold Canadian winter behind to vacation in Phuket [*poo-ket*], Thailand. It seemed like paradise, until 9:15 on the morning of December 26.

Troy was standing on his hotel balcony, when he felt a mild earthquake. No one seemed worried, so Troy ignored it. Then things started to get weird.

"About 45 minutes later, I noticed the water had receded from Patong Bay. We'd never seen it before, and we could hear people on the beach talking about it. You could even see fish flopping around on the beach, which was unusual.

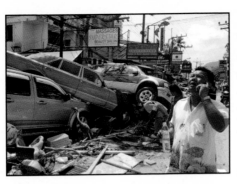

"Then I saw it — I noticed people craning their necks and looking out to the horizon. You could see a wall of water about three or four stories high."

The wall of water swept over the beach and just kept coming. It bent trees, picked up beach umbrellas and cars — anything in its path. Troy ran up to the roof of his hotel, but the water kept rising. ("It flowed up to the third floor, you could see it in the stairwell.") When it was over, Troy ventured outside. "It looked like a bomb had gone off."

A City Uncovered
SOUTHEAST INDIA
On the southeast coast of India lies the remains of the ancient city of Mahabalipuram. The city, a collection of temples, is a popular tourist attraction. But it turns out that there was more to the city hidden under the sea.

When the tsunami of December 26, 2004, battered the area, it did archaeologists a favor and uncovered two carved structures that had been buried in sand and water. Ancient stone lions and horses saw the light of day for the first time in many centuries, all thanks to the tsunami.

How Tsunamis Start

A tsunami starts with a huge shake-up of the sea floor. An undersea earthquake, volcano or landslide thrusts up the water above it and sends enormous waves spreading outward. The tsunami waves can travel for thousands of miles, but it is usually only when they hit land that they become deadly.

The seafloor rises and so does the water.

The bulging water fans out into waves.

The Power of the Ocean

No, he didn't see it coming. Yes, he did escape back through the doorway and closed the door in time. Whew!

TSUNAMI *Trivia*

ANCIENT TRIBAL FOLKLORE STORIES SAVE LIVES

On the small Andaman Islands just north of the earthquake epicenter there are ancient tribes whose folklore stories talk of "huge shaking of ground followed by high wall of water." This was an early warning system for them; these stories that passed from generation to generation taught people how to act in an emergency.

They went quickly to higher ground after the earthquake and saved themselves from the tsunami. Old stories saved them!

HOW OFTEN?

Ten or so tsunamis hit somewhere on Earth every year. Most do no damage.

WHAT'S IT LIKE FOR THE BOATS AT SEA?

They're invisible (the tsunamis, that is, not the boats). Sailors wouldn't notice a thing. The surface of the water doesn't move much as a wave passes because most of the action is underwater. It's only at the shore that the trouble starts. That's where the waves pile up into a wall of water.

HOW FAST?

A tsunami travels at approximately 600 mph (966 km/h) across deep ocean. About the same speed as a jetliner.

On August 26, 1883, the Indonesian island of **KRAKATAU** was the site of the second largest volcanic eruption in recorded history. The explosion and subsequent collapse of the volcano triggered a tsunami that wiped out 165 coastal towns.

Compared to a tsunami, this is just A Tiny Wave

100 feet

30 feet

The surfer pictured here is on a thirty footer, a regular wind-driven wave. When tsunamis hit the shore, the big ones can be 100 feet tall.

Is It Possible to Surf a Tsunami?

Out of the many unbelievable stories that came from the December 2004 Indian Ocean tsunami, was this one:

Surfer Martin Hambrook, 40, from Porthcawl, South Wales, was in the sea off the island's southern coast waiting for what he hoped would be a perfect wave.

Partner Vicky Maxwell, 42, and son Jai, 7, were watching from the beach as the horrific form of the tsunami appeared on the horizon.

"As an experienced surfer, when I saw the wave come, I realized something was wrong, but I couldn't escape because the surfboard was tied to my ankle." Despite the ferocity of the wave, Hambrook stayed on his board as he was carried over the sandy beach right up to the hotel.

He leapt off by a restaurant as the sea withdrew and a second wave, about 30 feet (10 meters) high, rolled in. The family then fled to higher ground where all three survived.

Rogue Waves

The photo here shows three men nailing plywood over windows. They had their backs to the surf, something that lifeguards will tell you is not recommended. The wave that crashed into them was far bigger than anything else around it.

1

2

3

Volcanoes

The volcano shown here doesn't exist anymore. It vanished — or at least a fair chunk of it vanished — during a spectacular eruption one horrendous day about 7,000 years ago.

In the months after the eruption, Mt. Mazama's dome collapsed, leaving a bowl-shaped crater. Rainwater gradually filled the crater to a depth of 4,000 feet (1200 m), creating a lake. Today Crater Lake, as it is now called, is one of the most popular National Parks. You can visit it in Oregon.

Our planet is Volcano Central. As you read this, 20 or so volcanoes are erupting somewhere on the Earth. The planet is studded with about 500 active volcanoes, and 50 or more erupt each year. Some volcanoes are one-day wonders. Others, like Stromboli volcano in Italy, have been erupting for thousands of years.

Volcanoes are holes or tears in the Earth's crust out of which hot lava, gases and ash ooze or shoot. When that happens, stand back. Way back.

A Volcano
X-Ray

It's tall, it's steep-sided and it's ready to blow. It's a stratovolcano, the most common kind of volcano on the Earth and one of the most explosive. A stratovolcano can shoot ash, cinders and lava skyward. And it can send a deadly mix of gases, ash and rock, called a pyroclastic flow, racing down its slopes at hurricane speeds. When a stratovolcano erupts, it's best to be somewhere (anywhere) else.

2 If a vent gets plugged with magma, the pressure builds until finally — kablam! The magma is blasted into ash and cinders and shoots out of the volcano.

3 Ash, cinders and molten lava build up over time, forming a cone.

1 Molten magma from under the Earth's rocky crust oozes up through one or more vents.

The Volcano Hall of Fame and Facts

Volcanic Bombs

Erupting volcanoes can launch rocks and blobs of molten rock into the air as "volcanic bombs." The crust of a lava bomb cools as it flies through the air and the bomb often turns teardrop-shaped. Scientists who study volcanoes up close like to wear helmets and fireproof "anti–volcanic-bomb" shoulder pads.

The Mexican Insta-Volcano

In February 1943, a patch of Mexican cornfield suddenly started belching out smoke, then lava. By the next day, a mini-volcano had formed. And Paricutin (or El Monstruo, as the locals call it) just kept growing. Today, the volcano-that-started-as-a-cornfield is 1345 feet (410 m) tall.

Black Smokers

Just about the weirdest life ever discovered on planet Earth is located on the bottom of the oceans. It's found at cracks on the seafloor that expose the molten magma under the Earth's crust and spew out ash and super-heated water. A very strange ecosystem has evolved beside these cracks, made up of horror-movie kinds of things that no one has seen at the surface. They get their energy not from the sun but from the hot chemical-filled water that rises from the cracks. Should the sun ever blink out, the life forms with the best chance of survival will be life that has evolved down here.

Airplanes and Volcanoes

In 1982, an eruption in Galunggung, West Java, threw volcanic ash more than 25,000 feet (7600 m) into the air. The engines on two jetliners flying over the eruption conked out in the cloud of ash, and both planes fell thousands of feet before the pilots were able to re-start them, narrowly avoiding a tragedy. Because of such dangers, airspace over active volcanoes is off-limits to commercial aircraft.

Nobody Got Hurt

This abandoned school bus was swallowed by lava flowing from a Hawaiian volcano. Some lava flows easily, while other lava is thick and gooey. The temperature of lava varies, depending on its chemical composition, but it can reach 2000°F (1100°C).

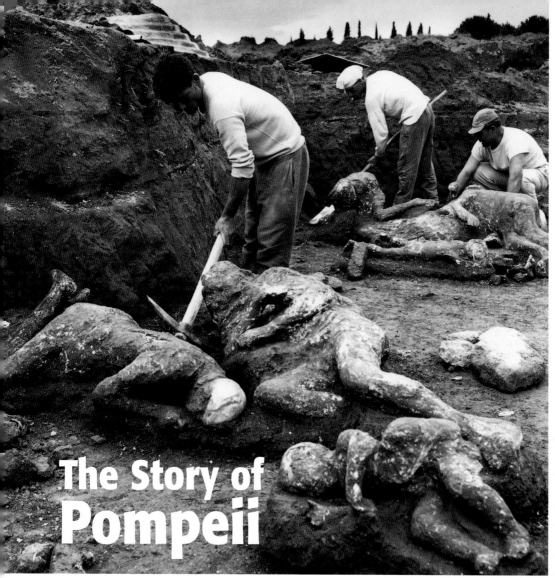

The Story of Pompeii

These are not the bodies of Pompeii's victims, but modern plaster casts. They were created by archaeologists who poured plaster into cavities left by the actual bodies.

In the year 79 AD, Pompeii was a village near Mount Vesuvius, on the coast on Italy. When Mt. Vesuvius erupted on August 25th of that year, the town and 3,360 people in it were wiped out.

Many inhabitants were suffocated by poisonous fumes as they fled their homes, and then covered with a layer of ash and mud. Over the years, their bodies decayed, leaving only bones and body-shaped holes in the hardened mud. In 1860, an Italian scientist discovered a way to fill the holes with plaster. Hundreds of plaster casts have since been taken of the Pompeii citizens, some of them showing enough detail to be recognizable individuals.

Mt. Vesuvius has erupted several times since it blotted out Pompeii, and nearby Mt. Aetna is also still active.

ITALY

Pompeii

Messy Homemade Volcanoes

spoonful of baking soda held inside bag

water & vinegar in 50/50 mix

Note: Bag is closed and sealed before baking powder is dumped.

Do This Outside

- Fill 1/3 of a big (1 quart), re-closeable, plastic bag with a mix of water and vinegar (half and half).

- Now get a friend to hold a tablespoon filled with baking soda entirely inside the bag so you can close the bag with the spoon AND its contents IN the bag.

- Seal the bag. Do not dump the baking soda. Yet.

- Now dump the baking soda into the liquid. Put the bag on the ground (outside, please) and stand back. You have about 10 seconds.

The Story of Mount St. Helens

In March 1980, Mt. St. Helens in Washington State began sending out a message that it was no longer a sleeping giant. Earthquakes shook the volcano, which had been dormant for more than a century. Puffs of smoke emerged and its peak sunk, forming a huge crater. Most ominous was a bulge high on the mountain's north side. It grew by about 5 feet (1.5 m) a day.

At first, local residents were nervous, especially when they were ordered to evacuate. But as the mountain continued to rumble and grumble for an amazing two months, people demanded to get back into their homes. Except for a few daredevil news helicopters, the journalists also packed it in. And many of the scientists were sent home.

Then on May 18, a huge earthquake rumbled under the mountain and the bulge tore away, creating the largest landslide ever recorded. A fiery hot blast of gases, steam and rocks flattened or burned everything in its path. The heat melted snow and ice, sending torrents of water and mud down the mountain at breakneck speeds. A plume of ash shot 12 miles (19 km) into the atmosphere.

When it was all over, Mt. St. Helens was missing the top 1312 feet (400 m), and a good part of the rest of the mountain looked like it belonged on the moon. Ash from the eruption fell over much of the western U.S. and Canada. And the giant has not gone back to sleep. Rumbling and belching smoke from time to time, Mt. St. Helens continues to keep its neighbors on their toes.

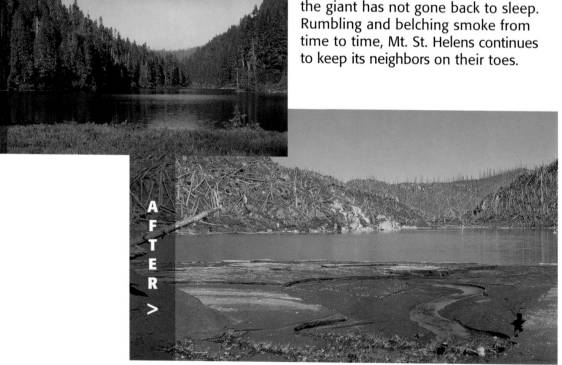

BEFORE >

AFTER >

"It was my wedding. And my sneakers were melting."

When Donna and Steve O'Meara got married, the bride wore sneakers and the happy pair arrived at the celebration in a helicopter. Partway through the ceremony, the bride's sneakers started to melt. No wonder: The O'Mearas were married on an active volcano.

The O'Mearas are hooked on volcanoes. Donna is a volcanologist, a scientist who studies volcanoes. Steve is an astronomer who studies how planets form, including their volcanoes. When they hear a volcano is erupting somewhere on the Earth, they grab their gear and go.

That's when things start getting interesting. They hike up volcanoes and hang out on the rim, studying and shooting the eruption. Lava bombs, scalding steam and hissing magma are all in a day's work for Steve and Donna. They're so nuts about volcanoes, they even live by one, in the town of Volcano, Hawaii, just at the edge of Kilauea volcano.

Donna and Steve at White Island Volcano in New Zealand, with a yellow wall of sulfur.

Floods

Most people describe a flood as simply more water than they want, in places where they don't need it. It's actually a good working definition since floods are hardly freaks of nature. On a planet that's already two-thirds covered with water, the fact that the other third gets washed over from time to time shouldn't come as any huge surprise.

Floods kill more people every year in North America than any other kind of natural disaster. Most floods come on fairly slowly as rivers crest above their banks. These kinds of "slow" floods are civil enough to allow time for residents to evacuate. But when the water recedes, it leaves behind a lot of mud and a mess that can take months to clean up.

In 1993, months of unrelenting rain led to a phenomenal once-in-500-years flood that overwhelmed 50 years' worth of levee construction in eight states throughout most of the Lower Mississippi River region. It was the most damaging natural disaster in modern North American history. Among the losers were the Quad City River Bandits in Davenport, Iowa, whose baseball stadium is pictured here.

At the end of the Great Ice Age about 20,000 years ago a giant lake formed near what is now Spokane, Washington. Half the size of Lake Michigan, it was contained by an ice dam that eventually broke under pressure. The water drained into the Spokane Valley at a rate of speed about 10 times the combined flow of all the world's rivers!

Early settlers in what is now Winnipeg, Manitoba, Canada, were warned by natives that the Red River was unpredictable and dangerous. Many regretted ignoring those warnings when the 10-year-old settlement became submerged in over 36 feet (11 m) of water in 1826. Other major floods followed in 1948, 1950 and 1997.

Residents of the small steel town of Johnstown, Pennsylvania, had always been aware of flood risks: The town was built on a flood plain. However, nothing could prepare them for the May afternoon in 1889 when the wooden dam just upriver broke and unleashed the waters of Lake Conemaugh. The rushing water wiped out the town, killing over 2,000 people and leaving many more homeless.

Q:
What Happens When You Mix Water and Dirt?

A:
You get MUD and grown men in suits, like Harrold Weinstein here, want to play in it, at least they do in the annual North Conway, New Hampshire, Mud Bowl.

In 1927 the Mississippi River overflowed its banks and flooded 27,000 square miles in 30 feet of water. The Great Mississippi Flood, as it is known, was the most destructive in U.S. history.

Flash Floods

Flash floods are hit-and-run rogues. They can turn a dry gully into a raging torrent in little more than a minute. They usually occur when a thunderstorm stalls out and drenches one small area. That's what happened in Kinlochrannoch, Scotland, where this picture was taken.

Riverfront Lot
Price Just Reduced By Half!

These photographs of a house caving in were taken during a flash flood in Tucson, Arizona, in October 1982. Flash floods are particularly common in desert country because of the nature of desert soil — hard-packed and free of plant life. The rain will hit and run if the soil is unable to soak it up.

The Hall of Flood Fame and Facts

The Forecast Called for Scattered Showers

It turned out to be a lot more than that. A flood that experts described as a once-in-a-century event nearly washed Rapid City, South Dakota, right off the map in June 1972. One woman found her car in a tree. Another discovered her house had floated to a brand new address. More than 200 people died. Today, in Rapid City, residents talk about the years B.F. (Before the Flood) and A.F. (After the Flood).

The Boston Molasses Flood

On January 15, 1919, an enormous tank full of molasses exploded at the Purity Distilling Company in Boston, Massachusetts.

A two-story wave of molasses roared into a residential area, killing 21 people and three horses. There are residents of Boston alive today who still cannot stand the smell of molasses.

The Missoula High Football Team (Class of 13,000 B.C.)

Missoula, Montana, used to be underneath a deep lake held in place by a monstrous dam of ice. In one phenomenal meltdown (15,000 years ago), the dam gave way and a flood of incredible

size inundated most of what is now eastern Washington State. The geologist J. Harlen Bretz, who first proposed this catastrophic flood theory, was widely ridiculed for it (geologists tend to think in terms of millennia, not Big Days). He was finally vindicated, years later, when giant ripple marks up to 30 feet (9m) high were found.

Putnam, Connecticut, 1955

This incredible photograph was taken August 19, 1955, in Putnam, Connecticut. Two rivers run through Putnam and in 1955 they were held in check by a series of earthen dams. Hurricane Diane and a torrential downpour proved too much for the old dams and they broke like a row of falling dominoes. The resulting wave of water came down Main Street like a runaway train. A factory in town manufactured magnesium, a chemical that burns underwater. When the factory walls collapsed, barrels of magnesium were swept away, exploding like bombs as they went.

Historic Floods

Guidry's Cajun restaurant is closed due to high water from the River Des Peres in south St. Louis on July 18, 1993. Most of this south St. Louis neighborhood was destroyed during the Great Flood of 1993. ▶

◀ High Tide

These kids are testing out their wet weather gear in the Piazza San Marco in Venice, Italy. Normally, the piazza is stone-dry square. But Venice is an island city at the edge of the Adriatic Sea, and when the tides rise, watch out. The Italians call it acqua alta, which means high water. In 1966 the acqua got so alta that more than 3 feet (1 m) of salty seawater sloshed over parts of the city, turning the Piazza San Marco into a giant wading pool.

"A Roar Like Thunder" ▶

Thunder is what it sounded like when the South Fork Dam broke and sent a wall of water smashing into the sleepy town of Johnstown, Pennsylvania, on May 31, 1889. Rocks, trees and chunks of buildings churned in the water, which raced downhill at 40 mph (65 km/h). In just 10 minutes, the downtown was destroyed, and many people were swept to their deaths. Then debris that piled up against an old bridge caught on fire, killing many more. When it was all over, the flood had the highest death toll in U.S. history. More than 2200 were dead or missing.

◀ Fire and Flood

In April 1997, Grand Forks, North Dakota, had a 500-year flood — a flood so big there normally wouldn't be another one like it in the next 500 years. From the air, houses looked like houseboats bobbing at sea. But the flood wasn't the only problem. Floodwaters knocked down power lines, which short circuited, starting fires in the downtown area.

You'd think all that water would make it easy to put out a fire. But there was just too much water. Firefighters had to slosh through chest-deep water just to get to the fires. When it was all over, nine historic buildings had burned down in a sea of water.

Ever Wonder What Would Happen If You Left the Sink Running for a Weekend?

A regular faucet can put out about 200 gallons (750 L) per hour. Leave it turned on for a weekend and, if your house is watertight and about average size, come Sunday night, you could be unlocking the door to 5 feet (1.5 m) of water.

This picture is a fake. Much as we would have liked to have really done it when we were kids, none of our mothers would let us try it and besides, nobody's house is watertight or strong enough to work like a barrel and really contain that much water. Disappointing, but it brings up an interesting point.

Water is heavy stuff. Ask anybody who's ever had to carry a bucket of it. Try to turn your living room into a swimming pool and you'll blow the walls out.

Credits

All cartoons by Elwood H. Smith unless otherwise credited. All table top and model photography by Peter Fox unless otherwise credited. All computer illustrations, touch-up, and reconstruction work by David Barker, except page 49 by Dave Pauly and pages 23, 33, and 38 by Brad Greenwood. The symbol 🖉 indicates substantial touch-up work or reconstruction done in Adobe® Photoshop®. Images are listed in clockwise order, beginning from top left.

Front cover: Alberto Garcia/Corbis/Saba.

Page 1: Photo Researchers, Inc.

Page 2: Arthur Harvey/*Miami Herald*.

TORNADOES Page 3: Cloud Gallery by Mary and Michael; James J. Abernethy (basketball hoops). Pages 4 and 5: Wade Balzer. Page 5 Illustration: Dave Barker; Bettmann/Corbis.

Page 6: *Miami Herald*; pre-tornado chicken Chase Swift/Corbis; post-tornado chicken Reuters/Corbis. Page 7: U.S. Navy/National Archives; courtesy of Teresa Bentley. Page 9 and 10: 🖉Mark Gormus/*Richmond Times-Dispatch*. Page 11: Wade Balzer, Leonard Lee Rue III/Science Source/Photo Researchers; Gene Moore; Dr. Scott Norquay/Tom Stack & Associates.

HURRICANES Page 12 and 13: NOAA. Page 14 Illustration: Jonathan Carlson. Page 15: courtesy of Lockheed Martin Aeronautical Systems; courtesy of U.S. Air Force Reserve; planes. Page 16 and 17: Photos © Chauncey Hinman. Courtesy of the Biloxi Public Library, Harrison County Library System, Biloxi, MS. Page 18: NASA (earth photos); 🖉NASA/MMI Corporation (red spot). Page 19: Steve Starr/Corbis.

EARTHQUAKES Page 20: Noboru Hashimoto/Corbis Sygma. Page 21: NASA. Page 22: 🖉globe

painted by Jean Doran Matua. Page 23: Illustration by Brad Greenwood. Page 24: Corbis. Page 26: 🖉W. C. Mendenhall, courtesy of the Department of Special Collections, Stanford University Libraries; 🖉Michael Schumann/Corbis Saba; Harrod Blank and Peter Fox. Page 27: Mark Aronoff/Corbis Sygma; 🖉Katumi Kasahara/AP/Wide World Photos.

TSUNAMIS Page 28: © Reuters/Landov. Page 29: AP/Wide World Photos; Courtesy of the Archaeological Survey of India. Page 30: © Jean Guichard/AlphaPix. Page 31: Terje Rakke/The Image Bank/Getty Images; Illustration by Brad Greenwood. Page 32 and 33: © David Fleetham/Photographer's Choice/Getty Images. Page 33: Boris Yaro/*Los Angeles Times*.

VOLCANOES Page 34 and 35: Painting by Paul Rockwood, courtesy of U.S. National Park Service. Page 36: Illustration by Brad Greenwood. Page 37: Photo Researchers, Inc.; G. Brad Lewis/Stone/Getty Images. Page 38: Bettmann/Corbis; Erich Lessing/Art Resource. Page 39: 🖉NOAA/National Geophysical Data Center. Page 40: Chuck Tonn. Page 41: © Stephen and Donna O'Meara/Volcano Watch International

FLOODS Page 42: © Ted Benson/Modesto Bee/Corbis Sygma; Larry Mayer. Page 43: Courtesy National Atlas/U.S. Geological Survey; David Brownell. Page 44: Laurie Campbell/NHPA. Page 45: Warren Faidley/Weatherstock. Page 46: courtesy of *Rapid City Journal*; AP/Wide World Photos. Page 47: 🖉courtesy of American Red Cross Museum. Page 48: Bill Greenblatt/UPI/Landov; Andrea

Merola/EPA/Landov; Johnstown Area Heritage Association Archives, Johnstown, PA.; Courtesy Department of Defense. Page 49: Daniel Brody/Stock, Boston; Telegraph Colour Library/FPG; Jeffrey L. Rotman/Peter Arnold, Inc.

Inside Back Cover: Les Stone: © Les Stone/Corbis Sygma

SPECIAL THANKS
J.J.&F. Market, Bernice Ruvkin, and Danny Yang.

MODELS Michael Berg, Laurie Campbell, Jason Chu, Alicia Edelman, Christina Foung, John Garcia, Dan Hafner, Darius Johnson, Natasha Johnson, Phylis Morrison, Kira Price, Myles Rowland, Josh Schneck, Jennifer Semanik, Clark Vineyard, and the El Carmelo 3rd, 4th, and 5th graders.

Development:
John Cassidy, Paul Doherty, Marilyn Green, Valerie Wyatt

Design: Kevin Plottner

Photo Research/Permissions:
Stephen Forsling, Marilyn Green, Lisa Timmins, Marybeth Arago